Solipsism and Stoicism

By Jason Brown

Dedication

To all of those I've loved along the way.

Foreword

Authors are routinely advised to write about that which they know, and so, accordingly, my first toe dip into the world of poetry, "Songs from the Heartland," focused on family stories, absurdities to which the response "you think too much" could be understood and forgiven, and frustration with the world around me - topics with which I am intimately familiar. (Maybe I'll someday write a poem about run-on sentences.) This second collection focuses the mind in a way that "Songs" never did (although there are still elements of lore, tangential thoughts, and irksome behavior).

The prologue recognizes the duality of the Midwest, with each section expanding on that duality by exploring the temptation and temperance; the depravity and discipline; the passion and patience; the bluster and balance that tenuously coexist.

The first section delves into the world of bad decisions, their consequences, and the sometimes understandable resentment that develops as a reaction to those consequences. The second section meditates on the enlightenment available to those willing to seek it in themselves and in those around them.

Together, these two themes - let's call them Solipsism and Stoicism - combine to inform the fatalism that comes from necessarily relying on the inherently unreliable whims of nature, forging a dichotomy of attitude that maintains sanity in an always unpredictable world.

The epilogue memorializes the social contract between the individual and the community regarding that relationship.

Prologue

Progenitors and Poetry

Mom came of age on a farm in the sticks.
Dad is from northern Appalachia.
He is a hillbilly and she's a hick.
So it made sense they moved to Iowa.

We all grew up in a small rural town.
Main street was wall-to-wall churches and bars.
On Saturday night folks could slam em down
Then on Sunday remember their north star.

Juxtaposition was part of the charm.
Indulgence led to indulgences and
a balance between control and self-harm -
"Too much" and "just enough" throughout the land.

Self-restraint and the seven deadly sins
Are Yin and Yang where my story begins.

Solipsism

15

Not My Problem

I'm too old to save you from your mistakes,
Principally those that are self-induced.
I cannot stop you from stepping on rakes
When your real bad habits have taken root.

If you vote for a dope or waste money,
You are the one that has to sleep at night.
Don't call me when life stops being funny,
After you realize you're in a plight.

"Managing up" is an inane concept
To absolve people of a consequence
That they are just unwilling to accept,
So they shift blame to others' cognizance.

Auditors get paid to point out your faults,
But I will watch you fail without a thought.

Coming of Age

There's a rundown farm near my childhood home
We all thought was an abandoned castle.
At eight years old, we were allowed to roam
And found a treasure hiding in its well.

We lifted the duffel with reverence.
Our neighbor had regaled us with its tales.
We unzipped in awe - not an utterance -
For sure if we got caught we'd go to jail.

But the promised reward outweighed the risk,
For all our questions would soon be answered.
We pulled one from the stack - stood at the brink -
There's no turning back, our fear we mastered.

The mag opened - down fell the centerfold -
And, oh my, it was a sight to behold.

Hunter, Gatherers

We trudged up the hill through freshly mown grass.
We then trudged back down the way we had come.
Late for a party because of an ass
Who out of the window had thrown some gum.

The tires had squealed and the rear end fishtailed.
The driver turned and questioned, "Who did that?"
We knew we'd been warned and now would be nailed.
Gum should be thrown out in the trash, not spat.

So there we looked for the offending mass,
Covering rows that were already hoed,
Grumbling under our breath, not daring sass,
Til "Eureka" it's found, the mother lode!

Hours looking for gum may seem a small thing,
But I've never tossed it like that again.

Dumb Luck

Racing a hundred twenty M.P.H. –
Down a two lane highway when three cars wide –
With the pedal floored and a topped out gauge –
Is not a great way to maintain your hide.

The Camaro and Mustang raced on by,
Against each other until they both saw
The Cougar approach, thinking he would fly
Passed both of them like a pair of grandpas.

They evened their pace so to block him out
Until the on-ramp added extra girth,
At which point the Cougar risked a blow out,
Stomped on the gas and took the narrow berth.

Three cars, side by side, no quarter given.
To this day no one admits who caved in.

Truth or Dare

Three drunk young men sat around a bonfire
Playing truth or dare with a cast and crew.
One dared another sit atop the pyre,
And he wisely demurred, sipping his brew.

The third said, "I'll do it, you damn coward."
And then picked up a sheet of scrap plywood.
He dropped in on the flames; his fear devoured.
He climbed atop with a desk from childhood.

He took a seat; flames licking all around.
Oohs and aahs rained down; fun was had by all,
'Til the sheathing failed and sent him to ground.
"Dead or just burnt?" the crowd started to bawl.

Twas a dislocated elbow – no more –
Popped back into place with minimal gore.

Stage Fright

Scaling balconies is faster than stairs
And gives the showman that extra panache.
An elevator is fine for the squares,
I preferred to tempt the fate of the squash.

It started out low – a deck here or there.
I didn't know what I had gotten into.
Before long I leapt to trees without care
And shimmied down like Santa in a flue.

Once – maybe – there was a couch fire involved,
And scaffolds reportedly unstable,
But from my habit I never evolved
Until I fell two floors due to failed nails.

No, a compression fracture is no fun,
And my balcony climbing days are done.

Ode to a Smoke

Your blood flow constricts, you get a light head.
Need for that first morning cig is no joke.
Rue scenes from last night, thank God you're not dead.
Somedays I feel like I'd kill for a smoke.

You wish to stop but your will is lacking.
From the second, you take a heavy toke.
Your body aches and you're coughing, hacking.
Somedays I feel like I'd kill for a smoke.

You need something to occupy your hands.
Third and fourth feel like they might cause a stroke.
You're an outcast now that they're all but banned.
Somedays I feel like I'd kill for a smoke.

The final cigarette is for the grave.
Your final reward after years a slave.

Social Media Addiction

"I seem to be losing my audience,"
He thought aloud to himself with concern.
Had he been too gaudy, given offense?
No, it's their fault. Talent they can't discern.

Still, how to get engagement numbers up?
How to slake thirst without looking greedy?
For sure, no one wants to see him pump up,
And shirtless pics may appear too seedy.

Marriage announcements and reveal parties
Are sure to rake in the likes, hearts, and stars.
Then again maybe something more artsy,
That doesn't involve crossing a bridge that far.

Oh, he knew he was chasing dopamine,
Addictive as any amphetamine.

Rhubarb

Git you a dad who won't call the police
When you done put the car in the rhubarb.
Git you a dad who will not ever cease
To crawl outta bed when you're at the bar.

Git you a dad with a good tractor winch,
Able to pull out your sixty-four Ford.
Git you a dad for whom it is a cinch
To hide your car 'hind where the crops are stored.

Git you a dad who don't ask no questions,
But wakes you up at the next crack of dawn.
Git you a dad who don't make suggestions,
Just 'spects you to work 'til that debt is gone.

It's true - you cannot pick your own parents -
So value one true as a knight errant.

RAGBRAI

The Register's Annual Great Bike Ride –
A drinking tour with a biking problem.
Ten thousand cyclists bike from the west side
To the east in a peloton column.

"Just because we slept together last night
Don't mean I want to ride with you today,"
Does not need to be taken as a slight.
It's just the *je nais sais quoi* in the hay.

For beer chugging contests and slips and slides,
Pork chops and chocolate covered bacon,
Come to Iowa in the summertime,
And enjoy four hundred miles to take in.

Athleticism's optional on RAGBRAI.
Just be ready to eat your share of pie.

Take a Number

Death follows life in the nat'ral order.
Nothing is alive that won't one day die.
Worrying only makes your life shorter.
Nothing can be done when your day is nigh.

That's not to dismiss burying a child.
Some things in life are not meant to be lived.
Outliving ones kids is rightly reviled
By the parents who will never forgive.

If there is a God - and I'm still in doubt -
The one thing I would like an answer to
Is what kind of supernatural lout
Asks innocent children to jump the queue.

Yes, death follows life - yes, it comes to all -
But taking youth 'fore age requires some gall.

Self-diagnosis

I took an online autism test today
And, as it turns out, I'm just an asshole.
I don't have issues with what people say
Or, per the test, sensory overload

But when it comes to social awkwardness
Ooh boy, yours truly tests right off the charts.
It's not that I don't like YOU, I must stress,
It's PEOPLE I hate with all of my heart.

So do not take it too personally
When I am avoiding your eye contact
Or pull an Irish Exit thoughtlessly
Or don't sympathize when you feel attacked.

You CAN take it personally I guess,
But I will not care, I must confess.

Waiting for Spring

I came home "sick" to watch opening day
But I didn't want to overplay it.
I didn't go full Peggy Ann McKay,
Just had witnesses to a coughing fit.

Home openers should be a holiday
For fanatics and casuals alike.
Nothing unites a town like a ball game,
And makes adults recall when they were tykes

And isn't that the point of holy days –
Community and childish wonderment?
Victory songs may now be how we pray,
With traditions passed down to the present.

Until then I will have to take sick leave
And try to convert the boss to believe.

Driving, Amirite

So, I don't know just who needs to hear this,
But those three car lengths will not change your life.
You don't want to know, but I'd be remiss
If I didn't point out that you're causing strife.

When you're weaving in and out of traffic
Not maintaining an assured clear distance,
The resulting mess could be quite graphic
And snuff out your corporeal existence.

Whether you are passing in the right lane
Or blocking up traffic when in the left,
Remember you can be a real pain
And that no one on the road is impressed.

The freedom rockets should give you a clue
That traffic does not revolve around you.

Flyover country?

When a storm happens near the Acela,
It is dubbed "Apocageddonarok."
When a storm touches down in Iowa,
It is dubbed "Monday" if any take stock.

It is not like we feel inferior,
But you do call us "flyover country"
As if the whole country's interior
Should submit to the haughty coasts humbly

The computer was found in the midwest.
Borlaug reinvented global farming.
The Ames Project met Roosevelt's behest
And ended fascism with just two bombings

You like computers, food, and being free?
Thank God an Iowan is on your team.

KonMari

Swedish death cleaning strikes as good reason,
because not any of this stuff sparks joy.
But if a match was struck in dry season
We'd be convicted for our fiery ploy.

There is likely some wheat among the chaff –
Some ruby's in Meatloaf's mountain of rocks –
Some collectible cars and antique crafts
At the bottom of this cracker jack box.

But good luck prospecting in this quagmire
Or getting accord on what to clean out.
As the years go on the piles gets higher,
Bursting at the seams, risking a blow out.

I don't normally have a turned up nose
But as executor I may bulldoze.

Fracas

This is a public service announcement,
When criming, leave your camera at home.
This is a public service announcement,
When rioting, you don't need Kodachrome.

In the wake of police brutality,
You might be tempted to commence looting.
Your trial will be a formality.
Graphic evidence there's no refuting.

"No face, no case," is practical advice
For all of you burgeoning anarchists,
But the simpler way to indulge a vice
Is to resist the urge to share your heists.

Some defend the right of social unrest.
Leave your phone when fighting for the oppressed.

Current Mood in Iambic Pentameter

For sure, no one wants to hear me complain
So I will try to keep this laconic,
"Fuck this fucking shit you fucking fucks! FUCK!"

Stoicism

Thermodynamics

You think it's simple to be this boring?
It is hard work to make life look easy.
Some bust their ass while the world is snoring,
To the uninformed their life is breezy.

The second law of thermodynamics
Tells us the world veers toward entropy.
One exerts force on the world's mechanics
To keep disorder and chaos at bay.

So when you see someone who's life is cush,
While yours is a proverbial hot mess,
Ask yourself if you've sufficiently pushed
The universe to avoid your distress.

It is hard work to make life look carefree.
And, no, it does not happen breathlessly.

Meditations

The best revenge is not to be that way,
So Emperor Aurelius opines.
In how you react you do have a say.
You can live your life by your own designs.

The best revenge is not to be that way.
When injured you have the choice to opt out.
You're able to reflect and walk away
Rather than become angry and lash out.

The best revenge is not to be that way.
Oh dear, this lesson is not just for you.
It's a reminder I need every day.
Mantras can reinforce a point of view.

The best revenge is not to be that way.
The best revenge is not to be that way.

The Way

The Tao that is named is not the true Tao.
Its purpose is limited when defined.
The nameless is the origin of all.
Desire takes over when names are assigned.

Wise men do nothing yet no chore remains.
Pupils work hard with always more to do.
Effortless action frees us from our chains,
While exertion keeps tightening the noose.

"Go with the flow, dude," isn't sufficient,
But there is a way to swim with the stream,
To accomplish goals and be efficient,
Without naming – even knowing – your dreams.

In the Tao you can see how the world works,
But name your goal and you will see God smirk.

Nothing Can't Be Fixed

You know what can't be fixed? Not a damn thing.
"Insoluble" comprises a null set.
Even Humpty, if he had a good king,
Would be cooked as a damn good omelet.

You know what can't be fixed? Not a damn thing.
Bike tires reinflate with one new tube.
Elbows can be set to heal in a sling.
Your too hot soup is cooled with an ice cube.

You know what can't be fixed? Not a damn thing.
Lost dogs are adopted; lost souls are found.
When illness wins, death's a new beginning.
Bit of wine and all your sorrows will drown.

Time heals all wounds, or so the old wives say.
From this we build – or rebuild as it may.

Y = 1 / X

Gius knows the horizon can't be reached,
Nor will the ideal society.
It can be approached but never be breached.
Utopia is like sobriety.

Three years in, and back to the starting line.
It is a race that will never be won.
Rather once you've won, you run one more time.
Or maybe it's a race that's never done.

Whatever idiom you tell yourself,
Control your step count where it matters most.
Whether it's the second, tenth, or the twelfth
Walk toward the horizon without boast.

Maybe sobriety's an asymptote.
Never quite there but close enough to note.

On Hero Worship

Acting like politics is a battle
Between your team's angels and mine's demons
Ignores that you're being led like cattle
While told to believe you are a free man.

Most pols have below average morals
And unimaginable shamelessness,
But they thirst for - they need - unearned laurels
And pray lowly sycophants acquiesce.

Spurn the trade of adoration-for-grift
And they remind you more of a neighbor
To pity than a seraph to worship.
More of a lost soul and less a savior.

Do not let yourself be swayed by false idols.
Holding power to account is vital.

Lessons Learned

Good judgment succeeds bad experience.
Bad experience succeeds poor judgment.
Wisdom's source is not that mysterious.
There's but one key to being triumphant.

To get good, you must start by being bad.
Beginner's luck - if real - is just that - luck.
No one got good without first getting mad,
Dropping more than the occasional fuck.

Yes, judgment is a skill that can be learned.
Like a toddler learns not to touch a stove
Only because his fingers have been burned,
Good lessons from bad choices come in droves.

Wonder how you get life to go your way?
Ask yourself what price you're willing to pay.

Who Tells Your Story

Live your life like your worst character traits
Will be caricatured in a memoir.
Do not leave your legacy to the fates
Or you will be remembered as bizarre.

The drunk, the con, and the degenerate
Will star prominently in some story,
But do not forget those who played it straight
Just 'cause conflict sells the allegory.

Open the business or donate your time.
Help with a big move or take in a stray.
Use lessons you've learned to help others climb.
It will all come back to help you one day.

Your legacy can't be known 'til you've quit,
'Cause attaboys are erased by "aw shit!"

They're Watching

Kids don't react to the news of the day,
They react to their parent's reaction.
So be careful about what you may say,
And how it impacts their satisfaction.

It is said that if you are not outraged
Then you must not be paying attention,
But beware of the culture wars you wage
And how you express your reprehension.

On par, each day is better than the last.
Although each year seems to say, "Hold my beer,"
No one informed wants to live in the past,
And we should celebrate progress with cheer.

There is still room to grow and rights to wrong,
But let children know we can get along.

At Sea

There's a feeling of untetheredness
That comes from completing the five-year plan.
Once the boxes are checked that governed us
It is a struggle to maintain one's brand.

"What will you do with all of your free time?"
"I don't know but I would like to find out."
"There are more corporate ladders to climb."
"You go ahead, I'll be in my redoubt."

When the chance for your retirement comes forth
Don't worry about how you'll fill your day,
But make sure you've established a true north
Or you'll find yourself with anchors aweigh.

It is fine to sail the wide open seas,
But do not forget the lane to your quay.

Life Comes at You Fast

The magical mystery tour of life
Has come to an end without much fanfare.
There is little bliss and even less strife.
Each experience says, "Done that. Been there."

That's not to say life itself has ended,
But the impenetrability's gone;
Universal secrets comprehended;
Conclusions of actions all but foregone.

I have achieved what I could when I could
and done what I wanted when I wanted
Most of the goals and dreams from my boyhood
Have been accomplished; I am not haunted

When called to heaven, life is picayune
Let no one say, "He was taken too soon."

Mindfulness

Just 'cause someone carries their burden well
Doesn't mean it doesn't weigh a damn ton.
Heavy loads are not always a death knell,
But carrying them still isn't much fun.

We all face the world with different skills.
Some can endure an emotional pain
Or rebound from an awkward social spill.
Others use humor to avoid the drain.

But we all need a break from our turmoil,
For outlasting cannot last forever.
We someday need someone to help our toil
Or risk our mindfulness getting severed

Ask for help – and offer it when you can –
When things aren't going according to plan.

The Weasel and the Pit

We all have things for which we should atone:
The white lie or the five-fingered discount;
The sarcastic "joke" with the hurtful tone;
The friend of whom you've taken no account.

But we owe the most to the broken hearts;
To those we swore ourselves before we left.
For an unrequited love may still smart
As it leaves both partners feeling bereft.

The high school crush has most likely faded,
But how about the called off engagement?
Can we pull through or will we be jaded,
Forever encumbered by estrangement?

It's beside the point who's wrong and who's right.
Just offer forgiveness and act contrite.

On Beauty

"Beauty is as useful as usefulness,
Perhaps more so," to paraphrase Les Mis.
On the other hand, so says the Duchess,
In the eye of the beholder, it is.

Concurrently utilitarian
And essentially discretionary,
One would have to be quite contrarian
To not see its use as arbitrary.

And therein, if I can offer two cents,
Lies the beauty of the word "beautiful"
It means what we want - against common sense -
Opinions don't have to be provable.

So find beauty in the world around you
And don't mind those who tell you it's untrue.

On Reason and Faith

Just 'cause I don't know the answer to "Why?"
Doesn't mean we should stop asking questions.
Rigorous inquiry can improve life
And avoid the horrors of regression.

But in life there's also a place for faith,
And acceptance and following orders.
Sometimes – and it is not always the case –
Submission results in less disorder.

Between these two poles, strike your own balance.
Choose what's important to you and what's not.
Set your own center. Fix your own ballast.
Decide for yourself the bounds of your thoughts.

Reason and faith aren't always conducive
But they aren't mutually exclusive.

Epilogue

A Community's Promise

If you can show up and show up on time,
We can teach you pretty much all the rest.
If you combine that with an urge to climb,
We can just 'bout teach you to be the best.

We don't know how to teach you how to care.
We can't want your success more than you do.
When you're faced with challenges and despair
Overcoming them will be up to you.

Tell us that you are in it to win it,
And we will give you the tools to succeed.
But if you fall the first time you get hit,
There is only so far that we can lead.

You bring the heart, the desire, and the drive
And we'll teach you the rest you need to thrive.